Rhode Island Civil War Monuments

A

PICTORIAL

GUIDE

R.N. Chevalier
Donna Chevalier

Rhode Island Civil War Monuments
A Pictorial Guide

By

R.N. Chevalier
&
Donna Chevalier

Rhode Island Civil War Monuments: A Pictorial Guide
Copyright © 2017 R.N. and Donna Chevalier. Produced and printed by Stillwater River Publications. All rights reserved. Written and produced in the United States of America. This book may not be reproduced or sold in any form without the expressed, written permission of the authors and publisher.

Visit our website at **www.StillwaterPress.com** for more information.

First Stillwater River Publications Edition

ISBN-10: 1-946-30006-3
ISBN-13: 978-1-946-30006-5

Library of Congress Control Number: 2017934531

2 3 4 5 6 7 8 9 10
Written by R.N. Chevalier & Donna Chevalier
Published by Stillwater River Publications, Glocester, RI, USA.

The views and opinions expressed in this book are solely those of the authors and do not necessarily reflect the views and opinions of the publisher.

Introduction

This book was born from two separate circumstances.

First, in 2011, our daughter Jasmine became involved with Hearthside House, a museum in Lincoln, Rhode Island that features docents, in period costumes, who give tours. During her time there, Hearthside House sponsored two Civil War reenactments including encampments and battles.

And then, in 2012, after I was diagnosed with ALS, I began using photography as a form of therapy. The job I had at the time of my diagnoses allowed me to travel throughout Rhode Island and Massachusetts. I soon realized that nearly every town I passed through had a Civil War monument. I started photographing the monuments to compare to each other. I quickly became awed by the craftsmanship of these monuments and, when my wife and co- author Donna saw the photos, she suggested we do this.

And so, it was conceived.

Dedication

To our daughter, Jasmine. Without your desire to be part of Hearthside House, this book would never have been created. We love you very much and are very proud of the person you are becoming. Keep up the great work.

Special thanks to Erinn Ballou Raimondi, whose friendly nudging helped to expedite the creation of this book.

I wish to offer a very special Thank You to my co- author, and my wife, Donna. You have put up with all my eccentricities and mood changes throughout the years and throughout my illness. I try to tell you just how much I truly love you and appreciate you every day. You are my life... forever.

Contents

Sullivan Ballou 2

Barrington 4

Bristol 6

Lincoln 8

George W. Olney 10

Newport 12

North Kingstown 14

Newport Artillery Museum 16

Pawtucket 18

George T. Cranston 24

Providence 26

Providence Civil War Memorials 30

South Kingstown 32

Woonsocket 34

Veterans' Memorial Museum 36

Rhode Island Civil War Memorials 38

Other Collections 42

Rhode Island Historical Resources 43

Research Resources 44

Sullivan Ballou

Sullivan Ballou was born in Smithfield, Rhode Island in 1829. His family moved to New York shortly after his birth. He came back to Rhode Island to attend Brown University in 1848. He left Brown in 1850 to attend National Law School in New York.

Sullivan was admitted to the RI bar in 1853. He worked at several firms, as well as on his own, while serving in the House of Representatives in 1857, acting as House Speaker.

He married Sarah Hart Shumway in October 1855 and had two sons. He was a man known for his integrity, honesty, and his deep love of country.

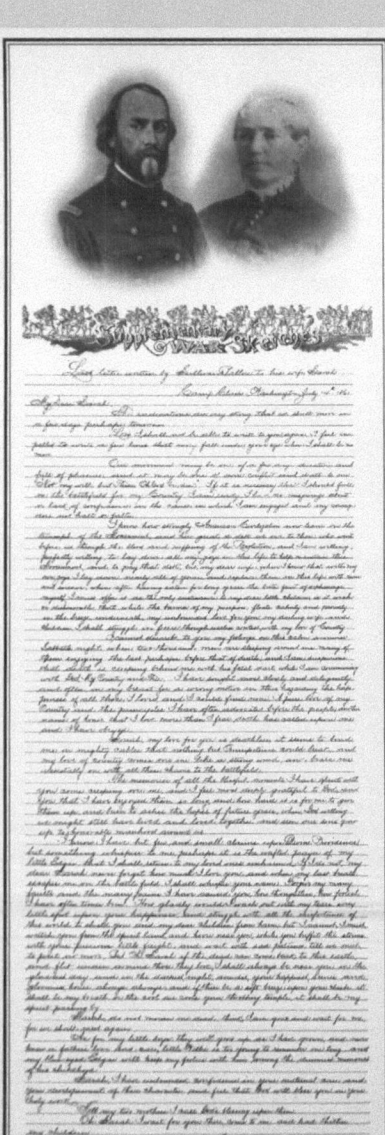

When Colonel John Slocum came to form the 2nd Regiment, Sullivan signed up. Because of his prominence, Ballou was given the rank of major, even though he had no military training. He went to war even though he felt he would not survive long.

Major Sullivan Ballou was killed at the 1st Battle of Bull Run on 28 July 1861 at the age of 32. He was buried along with Colonel Slocum at Sudley Church. Captains Levi Tower and Samuel James Smith were buried elsewhere, close by.

Governor William Sprague, who was at the 1st Battle of Bull Run, went back to Manassas in March 1862 after the Union took the area. He led a 70-man team to recover the RI troops killed there a year before. Colonel Slocum's body was found where it had been buried, as was Captain Tower's. Major Ballou's body was not in its grave.

Governor Sprague soon discovered from at least three eyewitnesses that members of the 21st Georgia Infantry dug up Ballou's body, thinking he was Slocum, several weeks prior to the team's arrival.

His corpse was removed from its coffin and beheaded. The body was then set on fire in the hopes of taking bones for souvenirs. The fire had to be extinguished quickly because of the smell. His burned bones, as well as some tufts of hair and two shirts identified as Ballou's, were discovered. The major's head was never recovered. The remains of Captain Smith were not recovered.

The bodies and belongings of Slocum, Ballou and Tower were brought back to RI by the governor. Found in Ballou's belongings was a letter he wrote to his wife, Sarah, but never mailed.

The now famous letter was so moving that it was, at some point shortly after its discovery, copied with slight variations. These letters are known as "original copies," of which five are known to exist. The Rhode Island Historical Society is in possession of one of these letters. The letter was read aloud in a 1990's PBS documentary series about the Civil War.

Civil War Monuments of Rhode Island

Sullivan Ballou was laid to rest in Swan Point Cemetery in Providence, as was Colonel Slocum. For Ballou alone, his funeral escort was a battalion of infantry consisting of the Woonsocket Guard, one company, Woonsocket National Guard, one company and Pawtucket National Guard, two companies.

When Sarah applied for her husband's government pension, her city of residence was listed as Woonsocket. She later moved to New Jersey, where their youngest son lived, sometime before her death in 1917. She is buried beside her husband in Swan Point Cemetery.

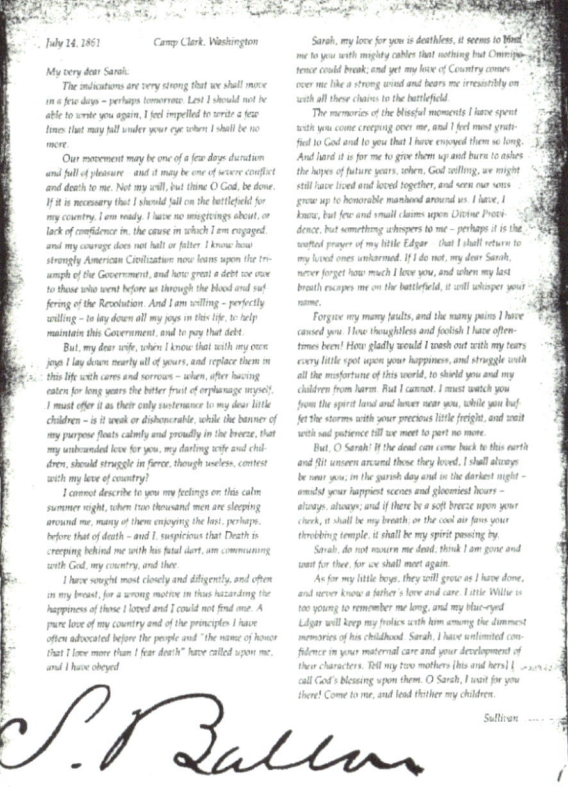

Opposite Page
A copy of the Sullivan Ballou letter created as a fundraiser for the Central Falls Public Library. The building that houses the library was the meeting hall for the Ballou Post #3, G.A.R. This letter is still available for sale at the library.

This Page
Top left – *Page 1 of an "original copy" of the Ballou letter housed at the RI Historical Society.*
Top center – *Page 2 of the letter.*
Center left – *Page 3.*
Center – *Page 4.*
Top right – *Transcript of the letter published in a 1939 issue of the Brown Alumni Monthly Magazine.*
Bottom left – *Closeup of Sullivan and Sarah Ballou from the fundraiser letter.*

Barrington

This monument is located in the rear-center section of Prince's Hill Cemetery on County Road, next door to the Barrington Town Hall.

The monument is a 4ft. wide by 4ft. deep by 12ft. tall unfinished obelisk, and is made from gray Westerly granite.

The monument was dedicated on 30 May (Memorial Day) 1905, at 3 p.m. as part of the holiday ceremony. It was unveiled by Harold H. Smith, the 7-year-old grandson of George L. Smith, chairman of the monument committee.

The town of Barrington is unique in two aspects:

• Some of the homes in town were reputed to be part of the Underground Railroad, aiding escaped slaves to freedom.

• Some of the more influential townsmen paid between $5.00 and $500.00 to other men to go in their places. This well-documented list is part of the town records on display at the Barrington Preservation Society Museum located in the town library.

Of the 51 men from Barrington who went to fight in the war, 11 did not come home alive.

Barrington Honor Roll

Ashworth, William
Barnes, Samuel A.
Chedell, Joseph A.
Drown, William A.
Gardner, Charles G.
Mathewson, John B.
Peck, Edwin B.
Peck, Noah A.
Richmond, George W.
Webb, William C.
Whitcomb, Lyman

Opposite page:
Top – *Front view of the obelisk showing some of the 41 grave markers.*
Center – *Grave markers to the left of the monument.*
Bottom – *Grave markers to the right of the monument.*

This page:
Top left – *The face of the monument.*
Top right – *Close-up of the monument.*
Center – *Opposite angle from behind.*
Bottom left – *Monument and markers from behind.*

Bristol

Upon entering the North Burial Ground at 1081 Hope Street, from the right entrance, one sees the full scope of the monument. From the mortar on the left to the mortar on the right, it's about 150 ft. wide with the monument set in the center. The section of the cemetery where the monument is located is called "The Soldiers' and Sailors' Lot."

The soldier is the work of sculptor Edward Pausch and stone cutter James Richards. The letter cutter was Abraham Datson and the polisher was Frank Mallon. The blue granite stone is from the Smith Granite Co. of Westerly.

The monument stands 35 ft. tall overall. The color bearer at the top of the monument stands 7 ft., 8 in. tall. He is standing with his left hand grasping Old Glory and his right hand grasping the hilt of his sword, in the act of defending the colors.

The monument was ordered by the state in December of 1901, erected in 1902 and dedicated on 30 May 1902 at a cost of $5,000.00. It is unclear what fort the two mortars come from; over 115 years of erosion and vandalism have caused the stamped letters of their identities to fade away.

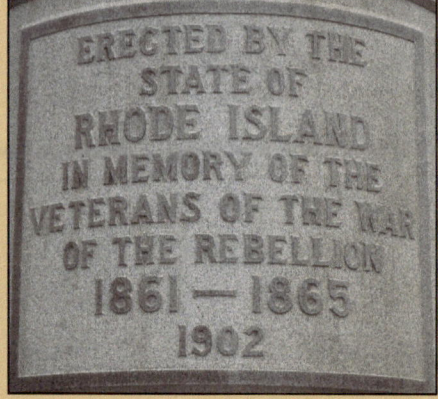

Civil War Monuments of Rhode Island

Opposite page
Top – *View of "The Soldiers' and Sailors' Lot" from the entrance of North Burial Ground.*
Center – *Full scope of the monument including grave markers.*
Bottom left – *United States seal engraved on the right side of the base above the stone mortar.*
Bottom center – *Dedication engraving opposite the nameplate.*
Bottom right – *Rhode Island state seal engraved on the left side of the base above the stone mortar.*

This page
Top left – *Close-up of mortar sculpture.*
Top right – *Base with nameplate and both mortar sculptures.*
Bottom left – *Close-up of the soldier showing the incredible detail work.*
Bottom right – *Close-up of the soldier's face.*

Lincoln

Located in the far left corner of Moshassuck Cemetery, 978 Lonsdale Ave. in the city of Central Falls, this monument was erected by the town of Lincoln and dedicated by The Ballou Post, #3, G.A.R. on 30 May 1888.

At the time the monument was erected, Central Falls and Lincoln were part of the same community, Lincoln being the agricultural region, and Central Falls being the industrial region. In 1895, Lincoln and Central Falls became independent entities. The separation was not amicable. The cemetery containing the monument fell within the new borders of Central Falls. Since, by 1895, Civil War veterans who passed away had been buried around the monument, the governing body of Lincoln decided to leave the monument where it stood. Due to the political climate of 1895, most of the records detailing the construction of the monument, at the time of this printing, are lost to history. However, the book, *History of Pawtucket, Central Falls and Vicinity,* published in 1897, contains a paragraph about the monument, reiterating the above information. It also states that the columnar pedestal is 12 feet high and the soldier is 7 feet tall. The monument is made of white Westerly granite and cost $4,000.00. A little known fact: The model used for the face of the soldier is General Ambrose Burnside, Civil War hero and former Rhode Island governor and senator.

The photos on the opposite page pay tribute to the talent of sculptor Emilio Piatti. Note the details still visible after 128 years: the hemline of his coat, the screws on his rifle, the veins on the back of his hands, the creases in his knuckles and his fingernails, just to name some.

Civil War Monuments of Rhode Island

Opposite page
Top left – *Dedication on the front of the monument.*
Top right – *Full scope of the monument.*
Bottom, left to right – *The four branches of the military, engraved on each side - Infantry, Artillery, Navy, Cavalry.*

George W. Olney

Like Sullivan Ballou, George W. Olney was born in Smithfield, in 1847. He was born into a good family but unlike Ballou, George enlisted underage and served as an enlisted man.

George's past relatives donated their land to form the communities of Smithfield, Lincoln and Central Falls.

The letter in the photos on the right (with its transcription below) is from an everyday solider talking to his father. He talks about everyday needs, the fact that he's in trouble, and upcoming conflicts.

Reading this letter is reminiscent of the letters I wrote to my parents while I was serving, as it should to any veteran who reads it. This letter is one in a series compiled at the Hearthside House Museum in Lincoln, RI.

This page:
Top – *Front side of George's letter.*
Center – *Back side of George's letter.*
Bottom – *Transcription of George's letter.*
Bottom right – *Photo of George W. Olney circa 1861.*

Gevners Island hospital
Newyork harbor Thursday Feb 16th 1865

My dear father I received your letter today and was very glad to hear from you I am well and I hope this finds you the same you said that my mother wanted to know if I wanted any socks and shirts I want them but I shant stay hear long enough to git them I expect to go to my company in to or three days you said that Langley rote that he expected to have a fight very soon I would like to be down their when they take richmond and see the fun I would like to be at home first about this time a good deal beter than to be fighting down at Petersburg you said that you wrote a letter to captain Thurber stating the case just as it was and he wrote back that I should be treated as well as any of his company that was good news to me for I expected to hav a cort marshal at the best and about his giting me a discharge I think he can git me one if any body can but you did not tell me wather or not you got that blanket and pak pak at the barracks in providence or not nesct time you rite tel me about it you said that you and mother was wel as usol and giting along comfobie I was very glad to hear it my mother wanted to no if I was very sick or not I am not sick now but are as well as cxman and want to git to my company as soon as posable sence I heard such good news from you I would give any thing to be at home I hav bin an this Island long enough a hav got sick of it I would rather be at my company a goodeal than to be hear now I know that I shant be cort marshald and when I git to the company if captain thurber can git me a discharge I shall be a new feler all together I shall feel as tho I could turn round and lick the rebels my self o if you knew how I want to git home you would do all you could to git me their as soon as posable but I think if I don't git a discharge as soon as I git to the company I shall in a month or two that is if general Sherman takes charleston as he thinks he will he has but all the rail roads connecting with Richmond and lees army cant git eny supplies from ther now and his men are an half rations and he sends to georges the only plase for them to send him supplies with out delay and grant is driveing him whar ever he meets him thay will clean the rebs up in a month or two if thay don't git their nigers in good working order pretty soon I forgot to tel that thare has bin a bounty gumper shot since I have bin in the hospital he was shot but a little ways from the hospital all the soldiers on the island was out their to see him they said that he gumped 17 bounties and if it had not bin for a hoar in new york thay would not caught him and thay are going to hang a spy and a pirat he is from virginy he and about a dozen of his band got on bord a steem ship on lake erie at one of her stoping plase and had arms consealed about them and about 9 oclock at night thay went into the crew and butchered them all and then they came acrost another ship and thay scuttled her and sat her adrift and since that thay have caught him as a spy in the state of new york and he is to be hung on the 18th instant I don't think of any more now but I hope to be at home with you in a short time you need not anser this leter for I shall be at the company in a few days

From your dear boy
George W. Olney

Civil War Monuments of Rhode Island

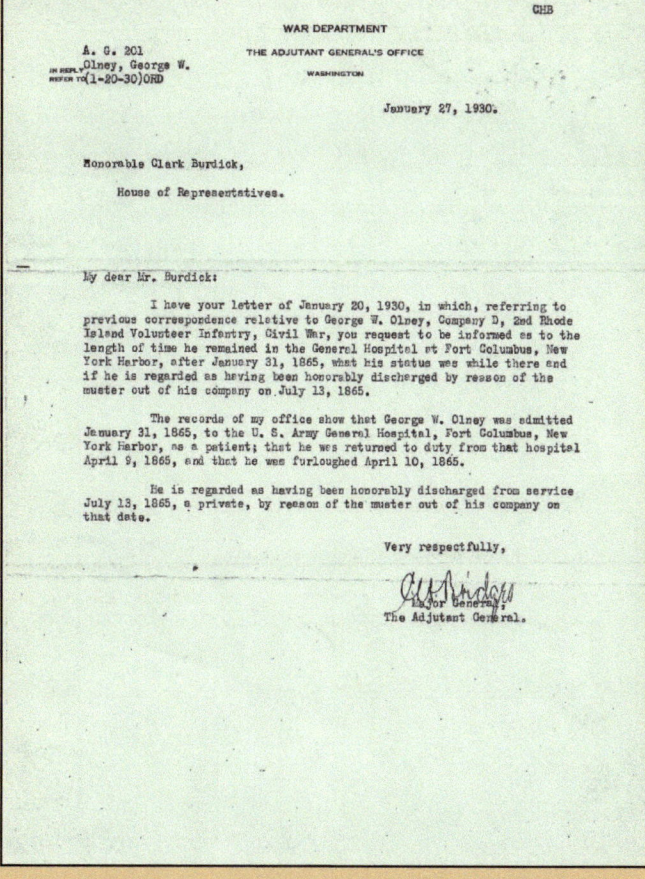

This page:

Top left - *Front and back of the envelope George's letter was mailed in. When he finished writing the letter, George took the folded paper and tri-folded it to fit the envelope.*
Top right - *One in a series of correspondences inquiring about George W Olney.*
Bottom right - *Color copy of George's photo, trimmed for framing decades ago.*
Bottom left – *Close-up of an 1865 postmark.*
(Letters and photos courtesy of Hearthside House Museum)

~ 11 ~

Newport

This monument, located in Congdon Park at Broadway and Everett Street, was dedicated in 1890 by the Charles E Lawton Post #5 Grand Army of the Republic. It was restored and rededicated by the Newport Cultural Commission in 2001.

The sculptor, William Clarke Noble, was a nationally respected artist. The red granite base is 11 ft. by 9 ft. 6 in. by 8 ft. 9 in. tall and comes from the Smith Granite Co. of Westerly. Included in the construction were: R. Roediger the letter cutter, and Mike Connell, John O'Connel and John Carney the stone cutters.

The bronze statues were cast at the Henry Bonnard Foundry in New York. Newport residents and Civil War veterans William Swinburne and Peter Dennis Melville posed as models for the 9 ft. 5 in. soldier and sailor on top.

The cost of the monument was $1,600.

Right - *Full view of the monument which faces the harbor.*
Left – *Close-up of the soldier and sailor*
Below – *Four bronze emblems surrounding the monument.*
Left to right: *Emblem of the G.A.R., located on the front, Calvary emblem, on the right side, Navy emblem, on the back, Artillery emblem, on the left side.*

Civil War Monuments of Rhode Island

Sculptor William Noble captured the essence of Peter Dennis Melville and William Swinburne in his work. Notice the details in the uniforms and equipment as well as the details in these young men's faces. After 126 years, these two men could shower off their makeup and go home.

North Kingstown

This monument sits in the far right corner of the Elm Grove Cemetery, 954 Tower Hill Road. It not only serves as the town's Civil War monument, but also a memorial to North Kingstown resident George T. Cranston (see pages 24-25).

The Charles C. Baker Post, #16, G.A.R. spearheaded the fundraising and construction efforts. Charles. C. Baker was the first North Kingstown resident to be killed in the Civil War.

The monument stands 25 ft. tall and is made from light gray Westerly granite. The base stone is 6 ft., 6 in. wide by 6 ft., 9 in. deep by 22 in. tall. The second stone is 5 ft., 11 in. wide by 5 ft., 11 in. deep by 18 in. tall. This stone bears the dedication inscription to George T. Cranston.

Atop the dedication stone sit 26 blocks of granite. Each block represents a post in the Department of the RI Grand Army of the Republic (G.A.R.). The front of each block is smooth and, in raised lettering, is inscribed with the name and number of each post.

The top stone bears the inscription "G.A.R. 1861 – 1865." The black granite sphere on top of the obelisk weighs nearly 1000 pounds.

The monument was designed and constructed by contractor S.E. Larkin of Westerly at a cost of $1,600. It was dedicated in 1898.

The dedication ceremony started at 9 a.m. with the arrival of members of the Burnside Post #2. They marched from the station (presumably the train station) to the G.A.R. hall, where the notes of preparation were read. At 10 a.m., a procession marched from the hall to Old Fellow's Hall, where refreshments were served.

The procession continued to Belleville Station where delegates from the other posts and guests of honor were met. The parade, now containing members of all the G.A.R. posts and camps and some forty carriages, marched to Elm Grove Cemetery.

The ceremony was attended by 3000 to 4000 people. Though the weather did not cooperate at the beginning of the day, it improved over time. During the ceremony, the monument was unveiled by Miss Annie Weinreich and Miss Gertrude Saunders.

One will notice that the block containing post #23 is missing from the monument. By 1897, when the monument was planned, the F.W. Goddard Post, #23, G.A.R. of Ashton, had been merged with another post due to decreased membership.

Opposite page:
The photo shows the monument, in its entirety, with all 26 post's names and numbers visible

This page:
Top left – *1000 lb. black granite ball capping the obelisk.*
Top, right – *Full monument with markers, from the front.*
Center, right – *The monument from the backside.*
Bottom, left – *Close-up of dedication block.*
Bottom, right – *Grave marker for George T. Cranston(see pages 24-25)*

Newport Artillery Museum

Above – *Union and Confederate uniforms with a 38 star American flag.*
Top right – *The Ames cannon, the last of the smooth bore cannons.*
Center right – *The black barrel cannons in the photo are the first rifled bore guns, the modern artillery weapon.*
Below – *An 1864 Confederate war bond.*
Bottom right – *An 1861 Confederate loan guarantee.*

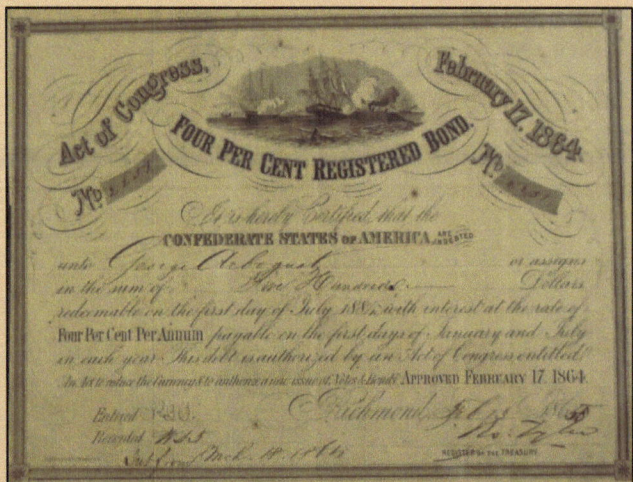

The Newport Artillery museum is located in the old armory building at 23 Clarke Street. The Armory was the home of the Artillery Company of Newport, the oldest military organization in the United States, chartered in 1741. The armory was built in 1836 and has a vast collection of military artifacts from all our wars as well as uniforms from the world's most famous military men. The museum curator, Robert S. Edenbach, Colonel Commanding, and his staff will take you on a provocative and entertaining tour through the history of wars and the history of the Newport Artillery Company. As for the Civil War, the collection covers flags to uniforms, swords to cannons and medical equipment to mundane items to souvenirs of battle, most of which was used by the members of the artillery company. Today, the artillery company is involved in Civil War and Revolutionary War reenactments.

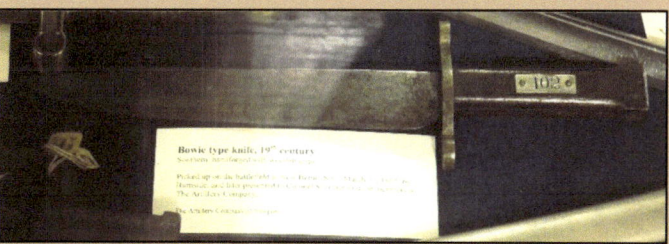

Top left and right – *Two photos of a medical kit used in battlefield hospitals.*
Center left – *A Civil War cannonball.*
Center right – *Confederate currency*
Left – *"Bowie" type knife picked up on the battlefield by General Burnside.*

Pawtucket

This monument is located in the Wilkinson Park at Main Street and Park Place. It was commissioned by the Ladies' Soldiers' Memorial Association after 11 years of fundraising.

The commission was awarded to William Granville Hastings and cast by the Gorham Manufacturing Company of Providence, RI, where Hastings worked as a sculptor.

The series of photos on the opposite page focus on the artistry of the sculpture for which Hastings is famous for. The sculpture, known as "Freedom Arming the Patriot" depicts the moment of decision when the farmer becomes a soldier in our nation's time of need. The sword is being offered by the goddess *LIBERTY*.

The sculpture stands 11 ft. tall. The base stands 10 ft. high by 22 ft. wide. It was dedicated on 31 May 1897 for a cost of $12,000.

The photo below shows the bronze relief on the back of the monument and the three photos at the bottom show the bronze reliefs as they appear on the front of the monument. The center relief is an artillery unit, commanded by General Ambrose Burnside, taking a bridge during the battle of Antietam.

The woman on the left represents *ETERNITY* and the woman of the right is *THE SCRIBE OF HISTORY*.

Pawtucket

This monument is located in the far left corner of Mineral Spring Cemetery, located on Mineral Spring Avenue in Pawtucket.

This is a memorial to the unknown soldiers

and sailors of the Civil War. It was erected and dedicated in 1902 by the Tower Relief Corps, an all-women organization chaired by Mrs. Emily F. Fish.

The base of the monument is 8 ft. tall and is carved from Quincy granite while the 7 ft. tall soldier standing at parade rest is made from Westerly granite, from the north quarry. The iron fence that encircles the monument and graves is 50 ft. 6 in. in diameter.

The dedication ceremony started with a parade kicking off on Exchange Street at 2:30 in the afternoon. The parade stopped at Wilkinson Park, where a ceremony was performed at the Civil War monument (see pages 18- 19.) A volley of honor was fired, followed by taps. The parade continued to Mineral Spring Cemetery.

Top – *Full view of the monument.*
Bottom – *Two close- up photos of the soldier's head.*

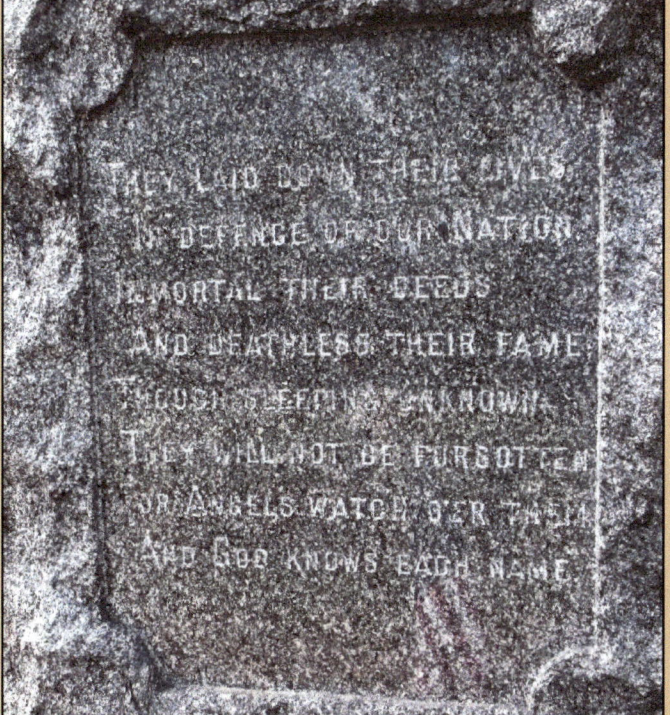

At the monument, the Tower Post Quartet performed, then the statue was unveiled amidst a ceremony of its own, including a poem written and recited by Mrs. Emily F. Fish. Again, a volley was fired followed by taps. The parade reformed and marched to G.A.R. headquarters, where they disbanded.

The inscription on the left, located on the back of the monument reads:

> They laid down their lives
> In defence of our Nation
> Immortal their deeds
> And deathless their fame
> Though sleeping unknown
> They will not be forgotten
> For angels watch over them
> And God knows each name

Top left – *Close-up of the statue.*
Top right – *Close-up of the soldier.*
Bottom left – *Close-up of the inscription.*

Pawtucket

This soldiers' and sailors' monument is in the St. Francis cemetery, Smithfield Avenue, on a plot of ground donated to the G.A.R. by Rt. Rev. Bishop Mathew Harkins. The lot is 36 ft. by 56 ft. and was given with the condition that destitute Union soldiers who were Roman Catholic would be buried there.

The "Soldiers' Shaft," as it was called, was dedicated on 30 May 1899 after 6 years of planning. It was unveiled at its ceremony by Miss Lottie Egan.

The monument was designed and built by Casey and Sherwood of Groton, CT. The *shaft* is 35 ft. tall and the top is surmounted by a standard bearer figure.

The cost of the monument was $4,450.00.
Top left – *Close-up of The Bearer.*
Top right - *Full view of the Soldier's Shaft.*
Bottom left – *Infantry engraving.*
Bottom center – *Artillery engraving.*
Bottom right – *Cavalry engraving.*

 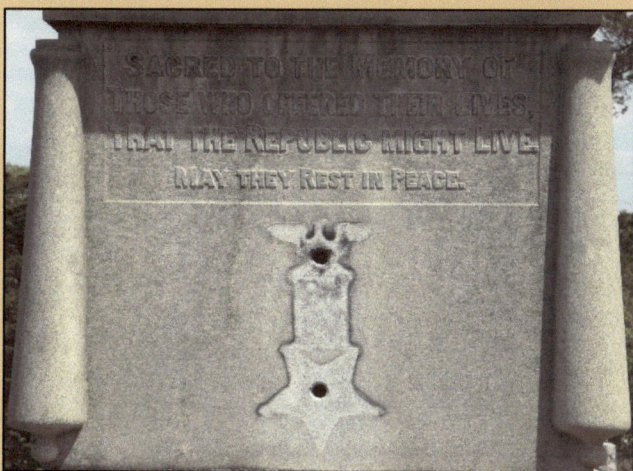

Top left - *This bird is located on the front of the column, directly under the soldier.*
Top right - *The United States seal, carved on the three sides surrounding the bird.*
Center left – *Navy engraving.*
Center right - *Dedication inscription and mounting holes and outline for the G.A.R. insignia. (a photo of the missing plaque is on page 12).*
Bottom left and right – *Close-up of the soldier.*

George T. Cranston

George Cranston was born in the Oak Hill area of North Kingston on 9 July 1844. He was educated at the old Swamptown school house. His father died when George was 13. He helped support his mother by working in mills and when the occasion offered, on the family farm.

When the call to arms came in April 1861, George, then only 16 years- old, tried to enlist but was turned away because he didn't have his mother's consent. When he turned 17 three months later, he begged his mother for her consent and she gave it. He enlisted in Company E, 3rd Rhode Island Heavy Artillery. He served for a year and was transferred to Battery, 1st U.S. Artillery; better known as General V. Henry's Flying Battery, where he served the remaining three years of his enlistment. He reenlisted in the 10th Massachusetts, also known as the Sleepless Battery.

His list of engagements include Fort Pulaski, James Island, Siege of Charleston, Baldwin, Cedar Creek (where he was wounded), St. Mary's Ford, Onester (where he was also wounded), Gainesville, Barker's Creek, Spotsylvania, Cold Harbor, Mechanicsville, Welden Road, Rome's Station (where he was captured) Staunton Bridge, Petersburg, 1st and 2nd Battles of Hatch's Run, Boyden's Plank Road, Bermuda Hundred and Drury's Bluff. Mr. Cranston was present at Lee's surrender, then mustered out on 10 July 1865 from Gallup's Island as a corporal of the United States Battery.

Upon leaving the Army, he worked on the large farm that he owned. In 1878, he started a general store and undertaker business in the same building. He ran the store until his death.

He was elected into the House of Representatives in 1881, where he served seven years. In 1888 he was elected to the State Senate, where he served until his death. While serving the Senate, his abilities earned him positions on various boards, the most prominent of which were the Board of Managers of the Soldiers' Home, the State Board for Soldiers' Relief and as a commissioner for the state's new campground. When the Charles C. Baker Post #16 of the Grand Army of the Republic opened, he became its first Commander. He served that position for 10 terms.

He then became Vice- Commander of the State Department of the G.A.R. and, in 1893, became the Commander of the State G.A.R. During his political career, he fought to better the lives of his brother veterans, as well as his hometown, North Kingstown. The Senator passed away at 12:45 on the morning of 25 October 1894. His official cause of death is listed as metastasis, the transferring of rheumatic trouble from the leg to the heart. His funeral was attended by Governor Dyer and many Members of the General Assembly. The State Commander of the G.A.R. , S.W.K. Allen and the members of his staff were also present. The huge amount of people present for his service was compared, size- wise, to that of General and Governor Ambrose Burnside.

George T. Cranston circa 1875

It was said George had a penchant for practical jokes. A story related by G. Tim Cranston, North Kingstown town historian, exemplifies this. George had a clerk in his store named Dewey. Every time anyone from the local clergy's household came in with an order, Dewey would mix all the beans, rice, dried fruit and tea in the bag.

When George found out he decided to teach Dewey a lesson. One day, George told Dewey he was leaving early to get a haircut and for Dewey to close the store. The last thing Dewey was to do before he left was to ice down the corpse in the funeral parlor (which was in the back room of the store.) George left, but snuck into the funeral parlor and moved an empty casket in place of the one with the deceased. He got in. When Dewey opened the casket, George sat up quickly shouting, "You white- livered cockroach, you! You would cheat the clergy, would you! I'll haunt you 'til the end of your days!" Dewey ran like a bat out of hell.

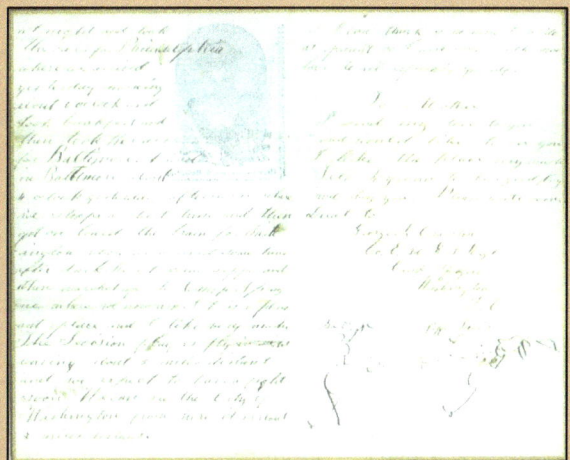

Camp Sprague
Washington DC
Sept 16th 1861

Dear Sister,
   I now take up my pen to write you a few lines. I am as well as (?) and getting along first rate and hope these few lines will find you the same. We were surprised last Saturday night to hear orders that we must start off immediately and accordingly we packed up and were off to Washington I have had a chance to see quite a bit of country since we left camp Sherman about 8 o'clock Saturday night and got on board the boat for South Amboy and arrived thereabout 10 o'clock at night and took the cars for Philadelphia where we arrived yesterday morning about 6 o'clock and took breakfast and hen took the cars for Baltimore and arrived in Baltimore about 4 o'clock yesterday afternoon when we stopped a short time and then got on board the train for Washington where we arrived some time after dark. We got some supper and then marched up to Camp Sprague where we now are. It is a pleasant place and I like it very much. The secession flag is waving about 5 miles distant and we expect to have a fight soon. We can see the city of Washington from here it is about 2 miles distant. As I can think of no more to write at present so I will with some love to all especially yourself.

To Mother
   I send my love to you and would like to see you. I like this place very much. Tell Lyman to be a good boy and obey you. Please write soon.

Direct to
George T. Cranston, Co. E, 3rd RI Regt, Camp Sprague, Washington DC

Above left – *Two photos of a letter written by George Cranston, to his sister, when he was 17 years- old. Note the Cartoon at the bottom of the last page. It is of him, George Cranston, shooting Confederate president Jefferson Davis.*
Right - *Transcription of the above letter.*

Providence

Located at Kennedy Plaza, this monument stands across the street from City Hall, having been moved to that location in 1906.

The monument was originally dedicated in 1871. The monument stands 43 ft. tall.

The granite section is 32 ft. tall. It is adorned with an 11 ft. tall woman who the sculptor, Randolph Rogers, described as "America at the end of the war." She is holding a wreath of laurels in her right hand and in her left, a wreath of immortelle. She wears the crown of liberty. The four soldiers, representing infantry, artillery, cavalry and navy, stand 7 ft., 3 in. tall. They were sculpted in Rome, by Rogers and cast in Munich.

Former Civil War general, now Rhode Island Governor Ambrose Burnside, headed the committee to build the monument. They chose local artist Randolph Rogers who lived in Rome at the time. The blue granite stone came from Westerly Granite Works of Westerly.

It was prepared and constructed by Providence architect Alfred Stone. Like a lot of the others, looking at the five figures on this monument, you would think that if they showered off their makeup and changed their clothes, they could go home.

Top – *Full monument.*
Far right – *Close-up of "America after the War."*
Immediate right – *Close-up of the face of "America after the War."*

The photos on this page focus on the four statues adorning the corners of the monument, midway up. The upper left is an artillery crewman. The upper right is a cavalry man. The lower left is an infantryman. The lower right represents the navy.

  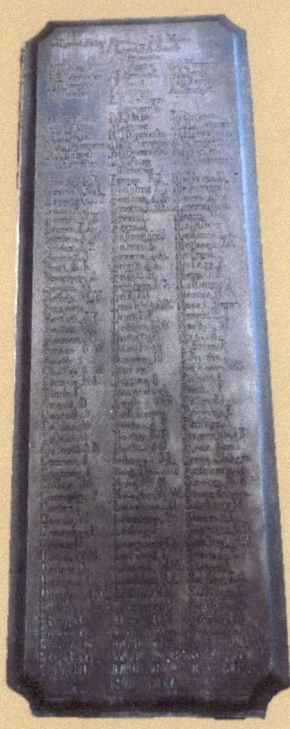 

Listed on these plaques are the names of the men who gave their lives, listed by units. Those units are:

1st RI Infantry	15th RI Infantry	5th Heavy Artillery
2nd RI Infantry	1st RI Cavalry	14th Light Artillery
4th RI Infantry	2nd RI Cavalry	Regiments from Other States
7th RI Infantry	3rd RI Cavalry	US Regular Army
12th RI Infantry	3rd RI Heavy Artillery	Hospital Guards

  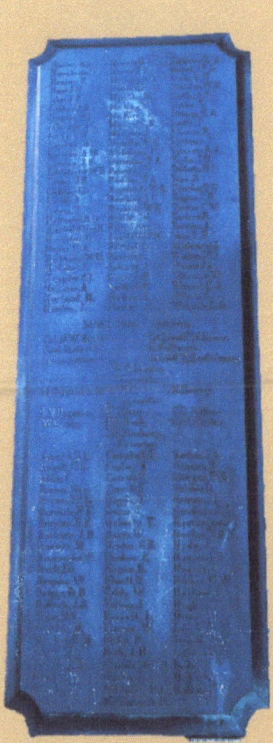 

Civil War Monuments of Rhode Island

The photos of the plaques spanning these two pages, from far left to far right as well as top then bottom, are Roll Call plaques. There are 16 that surround the monument. Twelve of these have the names of those men who died. The plaques are on the three sides of the four appendages extending from the four corners of the main shaft. The plaques of the women are mounted to the main shaft, in between the names. The four women represent, in order, WAR, PEACE, EMANCIPATION and VICTORY. The bronze plaques measure 7 ft., 3 in. by 2 ft., 8 in.

The total cost of this monument was $57,000 and 1,727 Rhode Island lives.

Providence Civil War Memorials

The two photos on the top are a memorial to Major Henry H. Young. The two photos in the center are a memorial to General Ambrose Burnside. These memorials are located in Providence, in a small park across the street from the Providence Civil War monument. Major Young is located in the east corner of the park and General Burnside is on the west side.

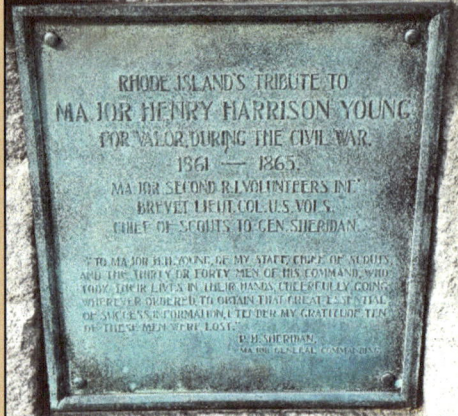

The Civil War soldier and President Lincoln are in Roger Williams Park.

They are on Hawthorne Street at the first rotary. They are so close that they are both visible in the above photos.

The memorial above, located at 1328 Warwick Avenue, marks the site of the encampment of the 3rd Heavy Artillery before moving out to the 1st Battle of Bull Run, where Major Sullivan Ballou died.

The memorial at left, attached to the Warwick Museum of Art, 3259 Post Road, is to the men of the 3rd RI Heavy Artillery, Company G.

Those from the 3rd who made the ultimate sacrifice are immortalized on the Providence Civil War monument.

The memorial, left and below, is on a small island at the intersection of Warwick Avenue and Airport Road in Warwick. It honors three soldiers from other states who are not listed on the plaques of the Providence Civil War monument.

South Kingstown

Top – *The monument from the front.*
Center – *US seal with wreath.*
Bottom – *Dedication inscription.*

This monument is located in Riverside Cemetery, near 161 High Street across from Town Hall.

This monument was the vision on Wakefield resident Daniel M.C. Stedman, who solely raised the funds for the project. Ground in Riverside Cemetery was marked in 1870. Raising money was a slow process, but the G.A.R. dedicated the monument on 10 June 1886. The base of the monument is 7 ft., 3 in. by 7 ft., 3 in. and stands 11 ft., 3 in. tall. It is topped with a drum, and draped by the American flag with two cannonballs, a sword, a canteen, a cartridge box, a wreath and a soldier's cap.

The granite came from the Smith Granite Company of Westerly at a cost of $3,300. In total, Stedman raised $3,308.48 from 321 contributors.

It is not known why the artist chose to cap the monument with an assortment of items. As a veteran, I can only speculate that since the drum is a "sound to war" and it sits covered by tools of war along with a wreath, I believe the only representation is... PEACE.

The names of the 64 men who gave their lives. Of the 250 men who left for war, these 64 men are forever immortalized on the four sides of the monument.

Below – *Two sides of the cap.*

Notice the details are still visible after 130 years.

Woonsocket

Located at Monument Square, where North Main Street, Social Street and Main Street converge, this monument is in front of the Stadium Building. The monument was commissioned in 1868 and erected and dedicated in 1870. It was the first Civil War monument constructed in the state.

On the front, near the base, is a dedication inscription. On the three sides around the dedication inscription are the names of those men, listed by rank from the town of Woonsocket who made the ultimate sacrifice during the Great Rebellion. Above the dedication inscription, an artistic piece called "The Trophy of War" adorns the next section of the monument. Above the "Trophy of War," embossed on all four sides, are listed eight major battles.

In 1868, the town of Woonsocket elected its first governing body. The first order of business for the newly- formed council was to commission this monument.

The contractor for the project was building contractor James Goodwin Batterson. He was the contractor for the Library of Congress in Washington, D.C. and, closer to home, the Vanderbilt mansion in Newport, R.I., also known as Marble House.

After 147 years in the elements, the incredible details in the soldier's hands and face are still so lifelike, he looks like an actor in makeup. The weariness of battle is immortalized forever in his hand- sculptured face.

Side note – While doing the research for this monument, all accounts, and there are more than one, state there are 39 men listed on the monument, 39 men who gave their lives. In the photos above, there are 40 names inscribed in the monument.

The dollar cost for this monument - - $5,000.00.

This page: Top left – *Full monument.* Top right – *Close- up of the soldier.*

Opposite page: Top left – *Dedication inscription.* Top right – *Officers killed.* Center – *Soldiers killed.* Bottom – *Close- up of the soldier to show the exquisite detailing in the sculpture.*

IN GRATEFUL REMEMBRANCE
OF HER BRAVE SONS, WHO, DURING THE
GREAT REBELLION,
GAVE THEIR LIVES THAT THE REPUBLIC MIGHT LIVE,
THE TOWN OF WOONSOCKET
ERECTED AND DEDICATED THIS MONUMENT,
MAY 28, A.D. 1870.

CAPTAIN.
S. JAMES SMITH.
LIEUTENANTS.
HENRY R. PIERCE.
ERASMUS S. BARTHOLOMEW.
SERGEANTS.
HENRY A. GREENE.
GEORGE J. HILL.
JOEL F. CROCKER.
CORPORALS.
THOMAS J. KELLEY.
JOHN FORD.

PRIVATES.
WILLIAM H. ACKLEY.
HENRY C. DAVIS.
JOHN HARROP.
HUGH MELVILLE.
LEANDER A. ARNOLD.
PATRICK KELLEY.
MATTHEW QUIRK.
ALBERT H. BALL.
EDWIN JOSLIN.
PATRICK O'CALLAHAN.
ABNER HASKELL, JR.
SAMUEL S. SMITH.
JOHN PRAY.
GEORGE W. STEARNS.
EMERY FISKE.
ROSWELL HATCH.

PRIVATES.
MICHAEL BURNS.
MICHAEL DRENNAN.
GEORGE RIEO.
THOMAS GREY.
WILLIAM FARRAR.
JOHN A. GORTON.
HENRY CONBOY.
ISAAC W. GREENUP.
DANIEL W. BURNHAM.
MARCUS L. SMITH.
HENRY E. TESTON.
BERNARD HOGAN.
JOHN BURKE.
LEVI SIMMONS.
JEREMIAH K. SHELDON.
THOMAS LEWIS.

Veterans' Memorial Museum

The museum is located at 78 Earle Street in Woonsocket. It is around the corner, less than a quarter mile, from the Woonsocket Civil War monument.

Above left: *Major Stephen Brown of Woonsocket.*
Upper and lower right: *The hat and jacket are from the 2nd RI Infantry. The jacket is labeled with the name Colonel Nichols. (The belt and sash adorning the jacket are, as of this printing, reproductions... for now.)*
Center right: *Close-up of the décor on the hat. Notice the button on the left has the Rhode Island state seal embossed on it.*
Below: *An 1865 $1.00 bill. Notice the name of the bank on the bill.*

Civil War Monuments of Rhode Island

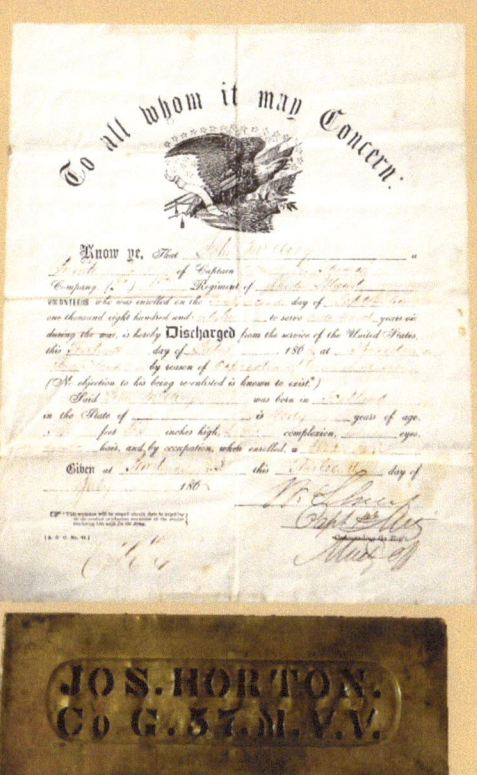

Top center: *The discharge paper for Private John McAvay, 11th RI, Company G.*

Above center: *Metal equipment stencil plate. It belonged to Joseph Horton, a member of Company G of the 57th Massachusetts, K.I.A. He is also an ancestor of Glenn Dusablon, curator and owner of the museum.*
Above left: *A Confederate sword and sheath taken as a souvenir of battle by George Oakes, 37th Massachusetts and another of Glenn's ancestors.*
Top right: *Canteen used by George Oakes.*
Above right: *A cartridge box that belonged to the 1st RI Light Infantry.*
Below left: *Payroll receipt for Captain Benjamin Hall, 5th RI, Company E, and his "servant" Toby Parker.*
Below right: *Several rifles used during the war. The top one is a Sharps Calvary Carbine. The one on the bottom is a Harper's Ferry Arsenal .58 caliber musket with bayonet.*

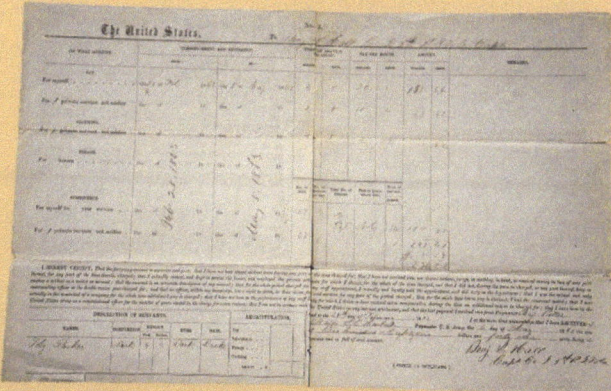
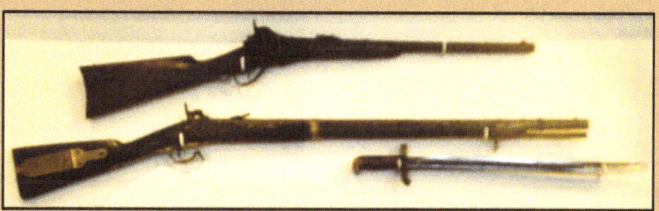

RI Civil War Memorials

East Providence City Hall, at the intersection of Taunton Avenue and Grove Avenue

 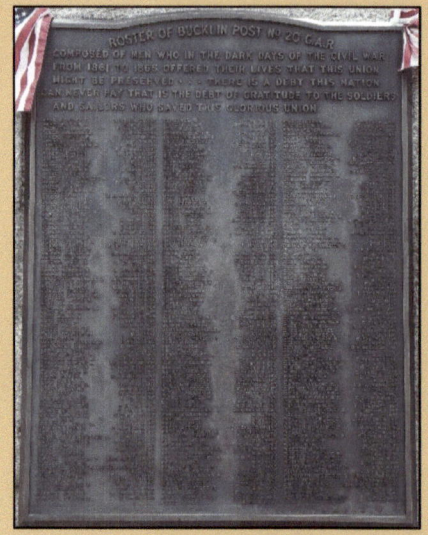

Little Neck Cemetery On Penrod Avenue in East Providence.

North Providence On the rotary at the intersection of Fruit Hill Road and Olney Avenue.

Civil War Monuments of Rhode Island

9 High Street, Warren.

Narragansett Town Hall
25 5th Street.

North Kingstown
Town Hall
80 Boston Neck Road

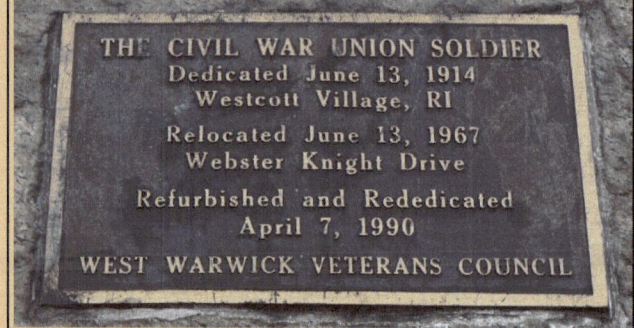

Top: *First Hopkinton Cemetery, Old Hopkinton Cemetery Road.*
Center: *Coventry Police Station, 1075 Main Steet.*
Bottom: *West Warwick High School, Webster Knight Drive.*

 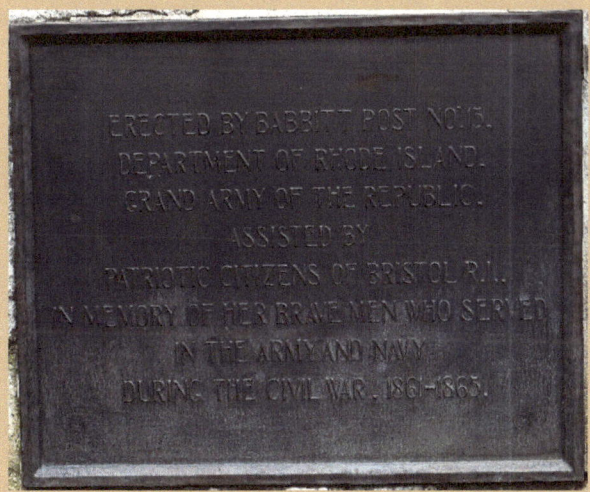

Top: *Bristol War Veterans' Honor Roll Garden, 400 Hope Street.*
Center: *Bristol Visitor's Center, 400 Hope Sreet.*
Bottom: *Manville Veterans' Park, 11 Parkway.*

Other Collections

Above right: Two photos of Sullivan Ballou's shirt collar, brought back from Manassas by Governor Sprague. It is preserved at the Providence Public Library in the Special Collections.
Above left: Background card accompanying Sullivan Ballou's collar.

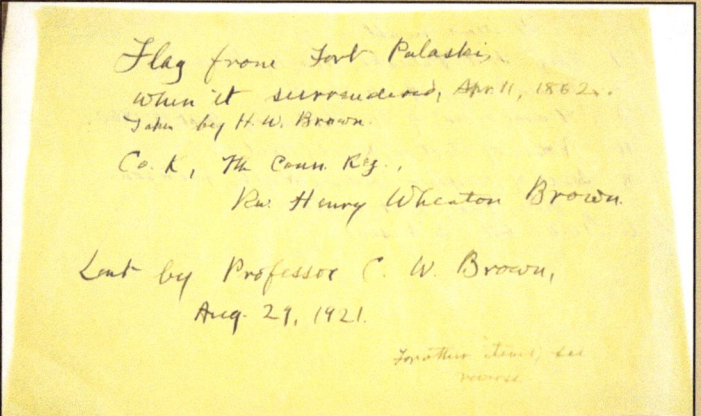

Above: Background card for the Confederate star.
Right: Photo of a star from the Confederate flag flown over Fort Pulaski, Georgia. This is also preserved at the Providence Public Library.

Right and Above: Photos of a Federal Cavalry saber, Model 1860. It was manufactured in 1864 by Mansfield and Lamb of Forestdale, RI, and now owned by a Providence woman. It has been in her family since it was issued.

Rhode Island Historical Resources

Clockwise:
Hearthside House Museum
677 Great Road, Lincoln, RI 02865
(401) 726 – 0597
Rhode Island Historical Society
Mary Elisabeth Robinson Research Center
121 Hope Street, Providence, RI 02906
(401) 273 – 8107
Veterans' Memorial Museum
78 Earle Street, Woonsocket, RI 02895
(401) 222 – 9025
Artillery Company of Newport
23 Clarke Street, Newport, RI 02840
(401) 846 – 8488
Governor Sprague Mansion Museum
Cranston Historical Society
1351 Cranston Street, Cranston, RI 02920
(401) 944 – 9226

Research Resources

Barrington Town Hall

Barrington Preservation Society

Bristol Town Hall

www.RI.gov

Central Falls City Hall

Central Falls Public Library

Lincoln Town Hall

Hearthside House Museum

Newport City Hall

Newport Artillery Museum

North Kingstown Town Hall

www.Wikipedia.com

Pawtucket City Hall

Pawtucket Public Library

Providence City Hall

Providence Public Library

South Kingstown Town Hall

Rhode Island Historical Society

Woonsocket City Hall

Veterans' Memorial Museum

www.History.net

Special Thanks

Kathy Hartley	Co-chair of Friends of Hearthside House
Tim Cranston	North Kingstown Town Historian
J.D. Kay	Rhode Island Historical Society
Robert S. Edenbach	Curator of the Newport Artillery Museum
Glenn Dusablon	Curator of the Veterans' Memorial Museum
Robert Scapini	Central Falls High School
David Stonestreet	Vice-president of the Barrington Preservation Society
Louis P. Cirillo	Bristol Town Clerk
Jordon Goffin	Head Curator of Collections – Providence Public Library
Matt Bennett	Pawtucket Public Library – Reference Department

About the Authors

R.N. Chevalier was born in Woonsocket, RI in 1963. He attended Lincoln High School after his family relocated to Lincoln during the blizzard of 1978. He served his country by enlisting in the Army then transferring to the Air Force.

He married Donna Fluette in 1993 and they moved to Florida. He is the author of *Are We the Klingons* and *Advances of the Ancients*.

Donna Chevalier was born in Woonsocket, RI in 1969. She graduated from Woonsocket High School in 1987 and Johnson and Wales University in 1997 after returning from Florida to attend. She, along with her husband, returned to Florida in 1999 for a second time. She gave birth to their daughter, Jasmine, in 2000.

The couple returned to Rhode Island with their daughter in 2004 and Donna went to work for "Corporate America." They are currently working on their next book, "The Civil War Monuments of Massachusetts."

www.ingramcontent.com/pod-product-compliance
Lightning Source LLC
Chambersburg PA
CBHW060757090426
42736CB00002B/66